M000195636

I ONLY HAVE MARMALADE

M. G. HUGHES

**THOUGHT
CATALOG**
Books

THOUGHTCATALOG.COM
NEW YORK · LOS ANGELES

THOUGHT
CATALOG
Books

Published by Thought Catalog Books, an imprint of the digital magazine Thought Catalog, which is owned and operated by The Thought & Expression Company LLC, an independent media organization based in Brooklyn, New York and Los Angeles, California.

This book was produced by Chris Lavergne and Noelle Beams with art direction and design by KJ Parish.

Cover illustrated by Maggie Stephenson (www.maggiestephenson.com). Special thanks to Brianna Wiest for creative editorial direction and Isidoros Karami-topoulos for circulation management.

thoughtcatalog.com
shopcatalog.com

Made in the United States of America.

ISBN 978-1-949759-36-5

*If you had the choice, would you pick
today up from the ground?*

*If the hour was an apricot rotting from the
inside out, the flesh browning through and
through, would you leave it to rot?*

Or would you make marmalade?

TABLE OF CONTENTS

Silent night,
Loud day—

You test
Me so.

And still I walk with
Medallion in my footprints.

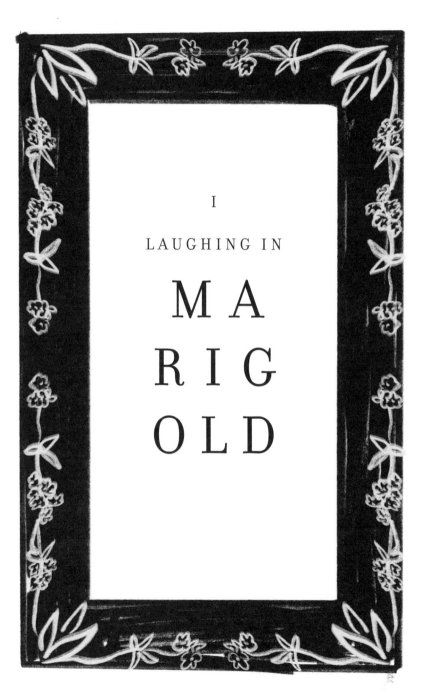

I

LAUGHING IN

MA

RIG

OLD

ERRANDS

Skip
Hop
Blue tank top
Was going down
To the Wig Shop
With Granny
Skip
Hop
Across the sidewalk
Was running errands
Under a wilting sun ray
Skip
Hop
Throw a penny in the fountain
Throw a penny and watch it grow
Skip
Hop
Think of a wish quick little Brown girl
Think of a wish quick little Brown girl

Make a wish for yourself grown Brown girl

ON BEING A HAPPY WOMAN

Little girl
Looks to
Cracked up sky
Looks to
Ancestors
Looks to
God
Looks to
Ancestors again
Looks to
Passing storm cloud
Looks to
Reflection in the water
Looks to
Cracked up sky
Looks to
That little girl once more

THE WOMAN WITH CLEAR COLORED INK

I could make
Entire mountains cry violet
All the canyons lose their guts
All the valleys and rivers speak
Their native leaf language just for us

But that would be too easy

On some days i just cry
over the way a lyric wrapped
its silk self around my shoulders

On some days

i just

let myself cry

SUDS

I bathed in nectarine
After taking the trash out
The feeling made me sleepy
And I almost drowned myself
On accident for having tilted my head
I slipped further and further into the tub
And after thinking on it I've realized there was
A metaphor waiting for me in the suds all along

But that's for me to keep and for you to figure out

in this land of
tangerine i stuck
my shovel in the
ground and planted a grey tree.
i needed something to aid my direction.
it was blinding, this land and its colors,
and in a strange way i viewed it as company.

i wasn't born with summer irises.

when i was born i proved brown.

ANCESTORS*

I stand before
A looking window
Looking out at six generations
I see a little girl jumping rope
I see her looking Brown looking Black like me
And while on one end there's a woman
Deep brown and four times
as wise as the girl and smiling
Dark curly hair no makeup no concealer
just natural beauty
On the left there's a polite shadow
that is black and see through
This figure does not look like a man or a woman
or anyone in particular
It's just a frame of a frame
(a frame of what could have been had I known)
But there's no doubt in my mind those are
constellations along the arms and legs

* *Originally written for Genre Urban Arts No. X issue*

You see

In the blackness of this void between
This person and me I do not see emptiness
I see the white crackling stars that flicker
to an unknown banjo song
I see the entire stretch of the Universe
I see today and yesterday
I see you and me
You see

I see Heaven looking over Pangea looking
over every grey lit street and village

MAGICAL GHOST GIRL

Where do I place
If I don't
Have that glow
You're talking about
If I don't
Have that gifted gaze
If I don't
Have that emerald thumb
If I don't
Have her motherland flame
Would you call it
Black girl or Brown girl magic
Would you call me
A magical mutt or a magical ghost girl
Not uncommon
Yet
Not impressive
Would you call me
A magical no-good or a magical nobody
Not invisible
Yet
Not doable

ARRHYTHMIA

Sometimes I touch
The area where my heart is
Because I can't take a full breath
It feels as if someone's pricking me

When I was younger my doctor said
The bump was a bone still growing but
It's still there still reminding me to love it
Like a baby bird left alone too long in its cage

CAMELLIA IN THE MOMENT

I was fourteen
When Camellia asked me
What's that is that blood
What's that scar on your hand
She was referring to my left
And what I told her was
Oh I got that from cooking
I accidently burnt myself
She didn't say anything
She had this strange look
On her deep brown face
You know the way we sometimes
Look at each other when we're
Absolutely sure we're not sure
That was Camellia in the moment
And when she finally said something
It went a little something like this
She said to me then in all lowercase

really

I just shook my head like that
I didn't say anything at all
But I was ready to confess everything
About how far down I was
About how I went to therapy
About how me and that me and that old lady
Had an awkward one hour discussion on *j e s u s*
The expression on her face made me think again
So I ended up sticking with the cooking explanation

(Because who would follow up on that?)

Looking back on it, though
I do wish I was her
If I was Camellia in the moment
I think I would've reached for my hand
Just to see if I would blink or flinch or cry
Over this new burning, flowering sensation

TANGERINE

Tangerine is on my mind
But I have no blanket to set

And there's a light in your eyes
I can't quite explain metaphorically

It's one of those things that's not actually a spark
It's just the way you look at me when you're talking

You inspire me to be like that
Not glad for everyone or everything but glad for me

For this life

PEACHES AND CREAM

Falling asleep
With nectar on
Your mind is a
Dangerous thing
You can dream
Sweet things but
You can never
Wake up with them

DANDELION

Dandelion you
Fly to places
I've only dreamed of

You make me
Jealous sometimes
With all your flying

But then again
You have no sail
You have no clue you're so high

So close to falling

FOR JULIUS

June I think I've
Fallen in love with you
But I've also lost my way
I don't have fancy frames
To display you in
And all of my strap dresses
Are thrifted from downtown
And I don't own a single bikini
Because I'm still unsure of my body
And I've never been big on brand names
Because I just don't understand busting out fifty bucks
And I don't have a perfect vase
To hold your yellow jewels of Helianthus
But June I think I've
Fallen in love with you

Am I in for trouble
Or am I still in learning

THE OTHER SUN

You said
Ghosts don't
Linger in this
Greening land
Because the
Combination just
Wouldn't make sense.
If ghosts were with us
They would have already
Taken us back to the Motherland
(And maybe me the halfway point
Between the United States and that one
Garbage patch that's twice the size of Texas
And floating in the middle of the Pacific Ocean).

Surely one of these ghosts would be
So polite to show us the way back to Africa.

Surely one of these ghosts would be
So kind to whisper to us the embrace of other Suns.

DAY TRIPPER

Let me guess
If I smell a flower
I'll fall over backwards
And realize I was wrong

I'll be double damned
If I stop and smell a flower
Because realization will be
That instant and that powerful

The scent will
Fuck up my nostrils
The flora catastrophe will
Send me flying straight to Pluto and back

Let me guess
If I smell a flower
I'll fall at your feet
And shout *o h m y g o d* for telling me to stop

GEMINI

Should've
Been watched over
Roses instead of Lily-of-the-Valley
Should've
Been lapis-oriented with
Invisible pearls hanging from my neck

Like a token gifted from lands of constellations

But I'm emerald
Through and through
I was not born to June
But I feel like I was
And although my knowledge on signs is limited
Sometimes I feel like even the stars are confused

If Alexandrite were a person I can guarantee you
Even she would not know where to send me off to

THE DEPARTURE

I've left rooms without
Actually leaving them

But on other occasions I badly
Wanted to hear the door slam

Now my exits are graceful
Even if that wasn't the plan

Even fire can look beautiful
When raging under natural lighting

SWEETENER

it was never about
cracking the sky open
or
letting all of my peaches blacken
or
preparing to take a stab at the night

it was never about these things because the bigger pic-
ture was more often a softer metaphor longing to push
its way past these stories of dramatic sunrising

sometimes the pain was as simple as remembering that
one time i felt like i was truly flying after she gave it her
all and before i was done with playground swings (the
time before i had yet to know words like freedom or
injustice or inequality) and while i don't think i'll ever
grow out of the natural habit of finding the likeness
between a lonely moon and a lonely afternoon that isn't
entirely singular but not entirely bright or citrine either
if it's enough to say i've grown past the reliance of
speaking sweetly to spare your part time loving ears...

i have

GRIEVING

Honeybees swarm
In places with no
Sign of bulb or stalk
And above me this
Oddly observant sky
Grieves with me over you
Its temperament
As the minutes pass
Ranging from
Cold to
Warm to
Subtropical

CHERRI

He showed
Her love
She showed
Him love
They went
Cherry picking
But his basket
Was already full
So full with another's love
His basket was
So heavy with loveliness
His handle was

So she and the tree left him

LOVING YOU ALL OVER

Grief is a
Roundabout
Sort of happening

If you don't
Miss them
On their anniversary

You'll miss them
When you think
It's just a daydream

Then you'll cry
And then you'll cry a little harder
And then everything will feel lovely

All over again
As if all of that was
Not once unexpected or exciting or particular

I let myself cry
Because
I've learned my lesson

FOR THE ONES ALSO
WHO'VE CRIED BURGUNDY TEARS

Closed your fist so hard you made red lines/screamed so loud the neighbors moved their blinds/screamed so loud the walls returned the sound and sucker-punched you in the throat/screamed so loud you got scared because that was the first time you heard your mother's islander accent in your own/screamed so loud you lost your voice screamed so loud you swore you'd never scream so loud ever ever ever ever ever ever ever ever ever ever ever ever ever ever ever ever ever ever again

banged a weighing scale against the wall so hard you made a dent and had to smooth putty over the area so the future homeowners won't ask who what the hell what the fuck when why how/banged your first on your own leg/(accidently) bumped your head on the crown of dawn...

it's not easy and it's real and i'm asking you to be kind to yourself

you deserve to hold your own hand today

We're little gods
Pretending
We're little Gods
Only we don't
Have wings
We only have
Skin and mortality

Don't chance
Yourself like that

These are
Perhaps times
For sailing
But if I told you
The sky is already
Soggy and doomed to the wind
Much like a paper boats do in true sea

Would you take some time
To reflect on what a bad idea the unanswered is

Or would you make a permeate
Conclusion over a temporary reversing of your tide

THE SHADOW LOVING FOLK

Hugging shadows does
More harm than good
I could see how
The grey imprinted
On him and them
And how their grey
Rubbed off on me too
Once the initial love was
Undone and repurposed

THE NIGHT GROWS A LIMB

No face
Navy eye
Navy to rib
Navy to navy
The night has
Grown a limb
It leans on
The fence
I suppose it's
Waiting for me
To believe
I'm free from it

No face
Navy eye
Navy to rib
Navy to navy
The night has
Grown a limb

See it
Leaning on
The fence
I suppose it's
Waiting for me
To turn around so
It can give its two cents
There is no luck
To be found in
Frozen-over clocks

No bribe
No sign
No face

Now is the
Main ingredient

UNCANNY

Sometimes I wonder
If a wishing star will fall out
If I scratch my scalp
A little longer than the last time

SKINNY LOVE

They said
Michelle
You need to
Put some meat
On your bones

That's
Why
You're so cold

They said
Michelle
You need to
Put some love
On your bones

Because of course
A skinny love is
Worse than no love at all

DARLING

You tell me
To love myself like you
But loving myself
Does not
Mean loving myself
Until it hurts
I can love myself
Until the love makes me cry
Until the love makes me think hard
Until the love makes me think about you
But because I broke skin
It was not even close to a lesson learned
It was actually an entire learning undone

Let me love myself
Like I know how to love myself
You tell me
To love myself like you
But loving myself
Takes meeting myself all alone all over again

At least two-thirds of the way

MY ROOM THE OTHER DAY

Wicker baskets
Quick bobby pins
Vitamin C tablets
Philodendron catastrophes
And every color of the rainbow

Except the first seven

PEPPERMINT

This is not
A love poem
But if you
Believe in
Red paper hearts
And
Pink passing times
And
Peaches so big you can—

That's a
Face left to your
Imagination.

I'm not a
Candy woman

I'm a
Young woman
Who just so
Happens to
Taste sweet.

THE BLACK GARDENIA

Lord
I never stayed long
With people my age
When I was growing up
I would go to her place
And from there we would
Often drive until we reached
A little blue house on a hill
It was through these experiences
I learned the beauty of long conversations
Brewing steadily and sometimes abruptly
But it was nevertheless always a good visit
So you can imagine how strange things can be
When the conversations switch from
The weather and the family and the how are you doin'
To pop radio and that one anime
And that one girl who said what now

Lord
I never stayed long
With people my age
I take too long to tell my side
I sit too proper too open sometimes
I like all kinds of music but Jimi and
Billie are my best friends
I like gardens and (supposedly) dirty beaches
And rose incense

Lord
I never stayed long
With people my age
Would you say I missed out?
Would you call me an old soul?

Or have I mistaken my white petals for heavy rain droplets?

Ever
Seen the
Sky go dark
In the middle
Of the day
Clouds appear
Out of nowhere
Full of beige tears
Winds become
Bold and human
Irises white but kind
Well this is growth

This is not the eye but mouth of the hurricane

THE FOURTH HOUR

I don't know why

For the longest time
I was afraid of the dark
I would put
My faith in nightlights
Out of this belief
The dark would play with my toes
But at some point
Greying rooms
Made me
Feel less alone

I don't know why

For the longest time
I was afraid of the dark
And then I let
The dark hug my shoulders
Out of this belief
Things like Morning and New were untrustworthy
And at some point
Greying rooms
Made me
Feel like I knew everything

I don't know why

It was
Chugging
Cups of sunshine
Until my tongue started to sting
Capturing
Every last bit of the year in a net
Until the holes expanded and burst
Clipping
Coupons that did or didn't promise
A full discount on this week or the next

It was all these things
And yet I remained trapped
In winter because I wasn't present

I was so determined I walked with my eyes closed

QUESTIONS

If growth is a progress
Then where do you say I end?
If progressing is a matter of here and there
Then what does setting boundaries look like in
Heaven?

On the day infinity comes knocking on my door
may I pick the color of my halo?

May I make mine glowing and light and lavender?

HILL ON PEYRI

Trees have
Cried here
But few
Stop to listen

Their branches
Swinging sullenly like
A broken holiday drugged up
With last year's freaky orange Jesus

DEEP CONDITIONER

Saturday
Morning
See the beginning
A god with an ombre face
As wide as time and space itself
Then see me
No robe
Just the
Water droplets
One egg
A half cup
Of coconut oil
A tablespoon
Of jojoba and black seed
Combining in
One bowl
Combining like
Two clear and orange worlds
Before sitting in my hair
For another twenty or so minutes

Or the minute I remember

ROOTS

Midnight aside I'm
Cherry blossom new
In a land of strange silk
The doves are not white or warm
But clear as sea foam, clear as glass
And the sea blushing
                    And faking it
                          And pinking twice over
Does not speak
Of foreign
Acts of unkindness
(The unwanted
Offerings her mouth
Was forced to intake)
But instead
A soulful drum song
I just know I'll know for sure
When I'm
Dead
Dead asleep

VIRTUOSO

The wind is
My keeper

The bank of
My bloodlines

And I found
My voice in its lift

In its net of
The wild and the woven

I grabbed hold of
A word and never let go

QUIET

Imagine that:
Being turned into
Projector for being
So soft-spoken.

My hands translate
The words I have trouble
Admitting to your face
But does that make me a writer?

At what point do
Hermits graduate
From their colorful shells
And become no-nonsense lobsters?

Did you know your fingernail
Has the capability of levitating
Four-hundred-year-old towns up
From the ground of which they set on

Stole

COMMUNICATION

I see you
Coming to me
Plains set in a
Perfect circumference
Lines divided
Dotted light and yellow
Winds spilling
Every lick of our family's secrets
Loudening
Loudening
Loudening
You're a tornado now
You're chasing me down the road now
You're telling me I should've never come

And then I wake up to a burnt orange window

CONTRADICTION

If rain falls
The moment I
Walk outside does
That mean I'm
Wonderfully in touch or
Wonderfully cursed?

Hearts with wings
Appear to have a
Funny way of following
Me out the door and yet your
Bonsai seeds never sprouted
When I planted them out back.

THE HEALER MUST ALSO BE HEALED

Black and silver daisies
Followed the walkway
Leading to your front door.

You were capsuled by winter himself
And I, looking in from the outside,
Burnt my fingers while attempting to bend the light in.

DAY GONE BYE

Knee to
The neck
Gun to
The times
Dead man
Dead woman
Dead son
Dead daughter   I said have we
Bullet to   Killed the
The door   Grandchild of Jim Crow
Pen to   Fist to
The time of   The sky of
Have we   Hands locked
Killed the   Like daisy chains
Grandchild of Jim Crow One two
Have we   One two
Killed the   One two
Grandchild of Jim Crow One two
                       Knee to
                       The Neck
                       Gun to
                       The times
                       Have we
                       Killed the
                       Grandchild of Jim Crow
                       I said have we
                       Killed the
                       Grandchild of
                       The translucent one

Out of rhythm
The heart may
Just stop
He said
He died
One breath at a time
And it makes me angry
Hearing him having to
Explain what murder looks like
Hearing him having to
Explain what Amerikkka looks like
Out of rhythm
The heart may
Just stop
And I say
Amerikkka will be killed alive
And be brought back to life as a result of turning
heads
Surely
Today
Amerikkka has been killed alive
And will be brought back to life as a result of all this
colorblindness

MARCH M*DNESS

The wildflowers were already
Throwing tantrums in the graveyard
And today is
The first day of spring
The first day of puking up 14k gold roses
The first day of digging large holes in the sky;

And I've been watching them
Find their way
Stain the hill with their little violet raptor wars
Hug his slab of forever stone like they're truly drunk
But it's really the coffins that do the talking because
A coffin knows missus spring better than any botanist

Better than any of these wildflowers of yellow, purple,
and pink

AMBIGUOUS

And now you're a guilty mosaic
Feverish shards
Square rivers no glue
One roof
Eight lands
Eighteen hundred ways to say blue

And now I'm a guilty mosaic
Bridging colors
Newfound borders no bone
On gold
Six eyes
Six legs but no way to overlap to call home

LIKE AN ANGEL

She tells you
It's because
You didn't pray enough
You didn't pray to
The Lord Almighty
You didn't say Amen
Loud enough when you kneeled
You didn't say it
You didn't say it
You didn't say it
Do you even pray
She asks
Then just before asking you
Why you're so skinny
She looks at you in a fixated manner
And without saying anything
She politely summons
Something spontaneous by way of her mind
And causes the area where your heart
Should be to become hot and funny and fluttering
Then just after confessing to her
That being petite was your mother's fault all along

She says
That couldn't be the only answer
So you just sit there reflecting on
What she just said about how
You probably didn't pray loud enough
You probably didn't pray loud enough
You probably didn't pray loud enough
You probably didn't pray loud enough
You probably didn't pray loud enough
You probably didn't pray loud enough

Then just before you leave
She tells you if it wasn't for the approaching blade of night
She would have sent you to a facility for daring to
even think like an angel

Your halo has now cracked in two
And out of the humor of the situation
The wind, suddenly too close for comfort, laughs wild
like it's a damn family reunion

OR YOURS

The knees and the upper thigh
Made for convenient canvases
Because it was easier to reach
For below than for behind.
Dizziness. Stillness. Repetition.
Obsidian was not a paint or color
But a disguise composed of cotton sheets;
The muse with ebony irises or the dark side of the
Moon
Whose fluids washed over my window.
Midnight. The strange waterfall: aiming and maleficent.
Daylight was a masculine bullet to the eye.
One peak from under the covers could kill.
So, like a hermit, I returned to this black well with
black water
Sourced partly from that same cut moon, partly from
that obsidian sheet.

Back
And
Forth.

Back
And
Forth.
Fingernail
To
Skin.
Fingernail
To
Bone.

Spilling burgundy had me believing
I was a talented colonist
Digging up expensive architecture;
discovering lost cells and pharaohs.
But there is no gold and no precious
goblet to be scratched out from this body.

Not even in illustration.

Golden girl and
She was Ebony
Her curls
Her reign
I didn't know her well
But I cried with her when
They told me she went Home
Because I know that longing
And I know

     I know

     I know

What it's like to think it's
Safer to take off than to take more time

Golden girl and
She was Ebony
Her curls
Her rain
I didn't know her well
But I pray she was allowed to be an angel
Loving her hair with coconut oil (just as they said she did)
Thinking about what a strange but wonderful thing it
is to be
Thinking about what a miracle a day can do when we
let the day cry with us

A TRAGEDY

They buried
Spring in a
Sarcophagus
At the base of
This ivory tower.

The line
Drawings:
Emerald.
The still
Face:
Blank, tan.

Stolen.

THE BITTER EARTH

this big blue bitter Earth
it's what we've got
it's what we've got to push with

not up against

NO LIGHT, NO DARK, NO MIDNIGHT

If I get a
Little more
Occupied
It will not
Be about
Sustaining
And if I get a
Little
Wiser
It will not be
Borrowed
And new fabric
Everything is a
Matter of everyone
And if everyone isn't a
Matter to everything aren't
You and I in a constant mode of
Meeting each other all over again?

Placing my faith
In myself is not the
Same as placing my faith
In myself when I'm feeling lonely

SHIT EGG

I tried to
Grab hold of
What I could of
The world and when
I finally felt something I
Realized what I was holding
Was my heart and my left lung
Squirming
Squirming
Squirming
Profusely
Like a worm caught in the rain
Dancing
Yet hardly
Making any real progress at all
So I let go
I tried to let go of
What I could of my precious organs
And when I finally had nothing I
Realized my hands were not stained
No red
No river
Not even a sign of dampness

I think it was a reckoning but then again
It could have been a bad dream
And while it could've been a nightmare
It also could've just been a bad day

SUMMERTIME

These hills know good and well
I'm not one to stay any longer than I should
They've put on their finest clothes
(You know the drill)
Gold and...
Gold and...
Gold and...

A little bit of red and blue to even out the politics
But I guess I'll be the one to fool myself in the end
These hills know good and well
I haven't sipped a single drop of crimson
They know I'm not drunk but they're hosting a party
anyway
(You know the drill)
Red and...
Red and...
Red and...

A little bit of blue and gold to even out the politics
But I guess I'm already a fool because I still haven't left

There is no such thing as summertime blues there is
only summertime madness

FULL MOON

I think the full Moon
Has finally caught me

When I turn all I see is yesterday
And there's a strange haze around today
Life is pink and fuzzy but not in that way
And the wallpaper has kindly reminded me it's hot out

I think the full Moon
Has finally caught me

When I turn around all I see is you and the fire
The smoke dragging the rain brought by chains
Life is getting pinker and fuzzier but not in that way
And the wallpaper has started to tell me what to be
sad about

I think the full Moon
Has finally caught me

LETTER TO APRIL

April they say it's time to love you
It's the time to be dizzy about butterflies
Laughing buds that are forbidden to say a word
Changing muses who are so stuck up they're beautiful
Wandering fuchsia petals that never knew their mothers
Praying hummingbirds who left the church a decade ago
Everything's pretty
Everything's wonderful
Everything's like a bright fighting
Because everything's trying to grow at the same exact time

And I don't know
On some days I just know

But I had a vase to fill with pretty nouns
So I thought I would sit down and daydream about
the close things

Like me and you and the daisy-filled ones

WHEN YOU CAN'T HOLD YOUR OWN HAND YOU CAN HOLD MINE

There was a day I was
Listening to a live album
Of Donny Hathaway
And I remember hearing him say
To the crowd before they started
Playing the first section of *The Ghetto*
That if he didn't rise the next day
Everything was going to be alright.

I don't remember if I knew why but I cried
Not long after because it meant so much more to me.

Of course the grass would still grow
And maybe these rooms would have been more lonely
But what would have happened if I took care of myself?

You wouldn't have stumbled across my words
And you wouldn't have known that I really wish I
could tell you that...

BLACK DAHLIA

Speak now or forever hold your peace.

But what if peace is knowing
Exactly where the bomb is placed?

If I acknowledge the work and the flame you and I
have left
Maybe the solution was to smile before turning the
other way.

We don't speak anymore.
You never cared to say sorry and you never said I
understand
But I'm happy for whatever flower your end of the fire
ended up becoming.

My fire turned into dahlias and now I have a summer
garden to love and appreciate.

Forever.

forgiving was
the only medicine
i had left in my
bathroom cabinet
and i'm yet again
all out of promises

there is a
flower to
be plucked
from every
black horizon.

DAWN

Honey quartz rising
Over
A middle-income town
Over
A middle incoming feeling
Over
A middle something loving

NOT A LEMON COUGH DROP

The words you and I
Force to decay
Inside of us that should've
Never been
Cornered
Shoved
Fucked
Absolutely south
Will either die before our time
And make us ill from remaining or
Very soon scratch its way
Up from our throats with
An intention to declare its civil rights

THE IMPRESSIONIST

Cover me
In watercolor
Shade me
In with brown
Carefully
Delicately
Like a poem
Left to bloom
Then allow
For the contour
Ginger and baby blue

A SOUTHERN CALIFORNIA TRYING

Excuse me
While I address
My many beachings
Have you ever heard of a California trying
Have you ever heard of a West Coast heartache
Have you ever heard of a little rhythm called passion

Nothing beats
More out of tune
Than a rising dreamer
Set against the clock
Set against the time we have
Set against the time we think we've already lost

The hour
Was a painting

And we were
The color palette

A CALLING OUT

When we passed each other
You called out once more because
I am the string and you are the tiger
With tan stripes set against white skin

Your hands are nothing compared to your eyes
Your eyes can kill without having to maintain
But not one bit of this is surprising because
You and I were born from the same concrete forest
with silver canopy

But without your claw
What would you claim?
Without your stripes of tan
What calling exactly would you stick yourself to?

Would it be one for loving roses or folding them
backwards over the dead grass?

STILL LIFE

Spring the truth is that
I wasn't ready for you at all then
When we first loved you showed up
In every month except the stunted one (January)
And now that I've seen you enough
I'm starting to get worried I've recognized you
I don't want to know you this way
I don't want to know you this way
I don't want to know you this way
But it's too late
I know your last secret
I don't want to know you this way
I don't want to know you this way
I don't want to know you this way
But spring the truth is that
Our last missing was two decades ago

I've seen your soul under
Gold twilight at every hour imaginable
And spring the truth is that
I wasn't ready for you at all then

My eyes have possibly wilted
I can't see color anymore but you're here

You made it

TALKING IS
HEALING IS TALKING

I saw Dippers
In my hurt
And hated my face
I loved
And unloved
But it was not that way
I said
Tell me

Do you know me

I could not look
Them in the eye
And when I spoke
I made my
Own father cry
But it was not that way
I said
Tell me

Do you know me

RHAPSODY

An orchestrated
Dream of
Melanin and bone:

Bare like rhapsody
Beneath the
Blue flowering moon.

WHEN LIFE REALIZED
ITS DRESS WAS A DAFFODIL

I looked up and realized I
Was looking at a contact list
Three decades old
Yellow and wise and frowning back at me
From the very top of her sunken-in closet door

HIS FLOWERS
IN THE SKY

If autumn was
The home hope
Was our roof.

If September was
The muse dawn
Was our carnation:

Our lucky
Penny
In the street.

TO A POET

Who spreads
Their love
Like a Sunday
Morning

Who magnifies
The hologram
Crimes of
Spring

Who hoists
The sun
Over
Splitting roofs

Who cries
Their soul
And
Their seasons dry

Who insists on
Harvesting metaphors
From the deepest
Rivers and walkways...

May your words
Deliver the honey
My own ears reject
During times of prolonging

MA BOUGAINVILLEA

Her children
Grabbed hold of the
Wind's offering hand.

Fuchsia
Through
And through

That side of
The block is
Now a greying paradise.

Low
Are the
Buildings.

Tall
Are the
Talkings.

Still they
Swear to
This very day:

Her children
Grabbed hold of the
Wind's offering hand.

THE TAN HOUSE WITH
LIGHT GREEN RAIN GUTTER

When enough time passed
I would drive by the house just
To see if the buyer would do as he said
He said he was gonna pull up the weeds
And build a house in the yard cause it was so big
And replace all the faucets and sinks and windows
He said he was gonna pull up the four-o-clock-flowers
And kill the guava tree and remove the birdhouse
She and I put up when I was nine years old
It was the same one she said I could take home someday
But I forgot about it and now (as it goes) I'm without
that little rusty paradise

And you know what none of that matters
When enough time passed I stopped the habit
I had to stop driving by the house for my own sake
Cause when I saw the corn stalks and white picket fence
I knew he was gonna make things look prettier
(unfamiliar) than it did

You can make a sad house look happy
What you can't do is force an old house to smile on its own

STILL, THEY LOVED

Mother loved his Daddy Mars
She gave birth to a Moon
Family lived in the cul-de-sac
The whole house cracked one afternoon

LATE MAY AS IN

Lemonade is not
A drink but a mood
Nothing is
Ever truly sweet
Ever truly like it is
When pink grapefruit is cut
When I'm all alone
With no one to share the slices with

(I can be selfish that way)

NEW DAY

I entered bronze and undone and with
yesterday's symphony
Time was never kind to whatever awaited
beyond the curve
But I decided to make something beautiful
with the heaviness
I took the big and the bad and the
unsweetened (the bitter sounds)
And forced them to sing my way not on time
but on my own time

Our conversation still stings
But all of this was always mine for the taking

All mine

An image:

me
daydreaming of
warmer places
in a warming place
all knowing of sepia
yet creased at the edges

FOR THE MUTE ONES
WHO WERE NEVER QUIET

Each time I think back
On that period of my life
The first thing that comes
To mind is the foul stink.

If you know what
It's like to lay so long
You start to sweat then
Maybe you know what I mean.
Tribulation can also be keeping quiet for too long

I ONLY HAVE MARMALADE

There's an empty jar
Sitting on the counter
But no one in this house
Wants to fill or claim it.
I've figured out pure marmalade
Is half extracted
During times like these;
The way we used to find
Gold in the private little moments
Stomach it or
Preserve it or
Hand it off to our neighbor
Is not the same taking-on we do today.

No.

Maybe it was similar but it wasn't as important.
Having marmalade these days is like having air.
If you can't manage to make peace out of mold
They're saying you're probably dead
Or that maybe you just believe you've choked
Or that maybe you just believe you've been living a
fourth awake.

WAITING

Next month's basket does not seek or excite me over coming to collect it. I've been here before and I know how this will turn out. The ripest fruit will go bad after a fly or gnat bites into it and the purest fruit will remain at the top of the tree all while the in-between fruit, the half-decided-upon, will insist on remaining halfway until the fourth week. Then every fruit falls. And then, as I wonder why this happened, the skies will go retro and allow my ancestors to laugh their worries out and over the world—the angels and God to release the dam of all of Heaven's urine. The result will be saffron. The meadow will be blazing cold with colorful rivers both shy and bold, tall and weary (as goes my allergies).

And then, as I wonder why the seasons must come and go like this, I will look at you and ask the fake million-dollar question.

Why?

BLACK CUMULUS

When I was in high school, I would draw clouds around my answers in math class cause I was bad with circles. When he asked me why I did this, I didn't tell him the truth cause I didn't think he deserved to know. I'm still like this. If you were to ask me why I cut into myself, or why I let myself feel that way, I would give you the short answer or nothing at all. And now that I've finally gotten a taste of what it's like to bare your soul I've also realized how dumb all this may sound. It's true that you know a little more of my story—and maybe you don't deserve to know me this way. But I guess you know all of that now, anyway, and how I once thought 0.7 thick white clouds were adorable.

Don't cry for me.

It's what we still respect as strangers that matters most.

When I fell
I landed on
Something plush
It wasn't my bed

I think it was Heaven

THE TIMES

Unfurling skies
Fertilized by
Unhooked daydreams
Like a million
Dandelions left to haunt
Like grey spirits
Unbothered by
The changing of
The tide of these tightening times
Unchanged but
Nevertheless becoming
Unbothered but
Nevertheless flowering imperfectly

Like a bullet aimed at a young cherry blossom

LAUGHING IN MARIGOLD

The tested memory
Of the teller;

The warm light
In the front living room.

The good times become
Good times when the good times
Have long passed us by and we find
Ourselves in a sudden state of reckoning

MARIGOLD TO THE BONE

When autumn wrapped
Her cheap fabrics around half of the equator,

When the sky
Was tampered by her nectarine pit of a tapestry,

We were all that.
We were marigold to the bone.

WHEN IN VALENCE

The cosmos pouring out
the last of their liquor
as the lapis morning
crawls out of bed on four legs.

FEELING

Give me that evening:
The kind of evening that
Moves in tones of butterscotch.

Give me that feeling:
The kind of feeling that
Forgives the hardest ribs of blues.

Our becoming was a drowsy
Late summer foreshadowing

A cliché

WHEN I WALK THE BEND

Drops of Venus were already growing up between the
Man's pants as he lay forward with his veins so blue
Bottle was empty and it always hung around

Just a little closer
Just a little closer
Like that was his first grandbaby

It was the only act that assured me he wasn't dead
I think back on that day sometimes when I walk the bend
The way his blues was his only company
The way the concrete was trying to French kiss him

I thought to myself then:
When nobody loves us the world takes over

MAPS

Flower shop
Next to
Liquor store
Across from
Another liquor store
One intersection away from
Police station
Across from
Library
Across from
Dollar store
Across from
Hair salon
Across from
Gas station
Across from
Bakery
Across from
That one stoplight

THE MIDNIGHT TREE

Come
Come
He says
Meet me
At the
Midnight tree

Let us sit under
The tree
Blacker than the night
The tree
Black and bright
Like October split open

BENEVOLENCE

Maybe it is
Not a matter of
Light and dark
Or chilly and balmy
Or
Micro and long form
Or
One thing and its opposite.

Maybe everything
Is made of poetry.

Maybe matter
Is a science of rhythm and blues.

FOR MARCH'S LOVERS

Easy as the wind
Tracing the lines of April.

Chilly as the touch of winter
Moving up and up and up May's thighs.

Warm as the opera of summer
Singing that strange watercolor into the night.

Loving under a thunderstorm

YOUR LOVE IS A HORNET

Not a pair of scissors
can cut all the way through
the silver edge gets caught halfway
your witch hazel toner and lavender guise
are all pretty pastel towels held before my eyes
one to be placed over my back
one to be placed over my head
peace shall
rise
rise
rise
like steam if i stand hunched over long enough
and love shall
gain
gain
gain
in its potency and its needle-sharp point once again
but not even his sharpened sword stuck in the rock
can cut from one edge to the opposite edge (i don't
think)
your rose petals and herbal momentums are too
organized

too extravagant for a day like today

YESTERDAY'S NECTAR

I remember us drinking the entirety
Of that year like sweet autumn nectar.
Day came to us in such helpful doses that
Not even the hummingbirds envied our stockpile.

Where does pleasure go when
Its white glimmering waters have evaporated?
They say everything returns to our ancestors…

But even the rain knows they'd spit out our black
and white affairs.

MOON-STRICKEN

Moon stricken
She plucked a
Corner of His
Silver quarter.

The color
Of the water
(Boiling):
Red as rose.

The canvas
Of the evening
(Unraveling):
Layered as a metamorphosis.

A PORTION OF THE SUNSET

You grabbed a portion of the sunset
And poured the apricot glow
Into a tall, sheer, canary colored pitcher.

The
Questions of
The hour:

Shall we drink
It now or
Freeze it for cubes?;

If ever frozen
Will the ice harden
Or run soft like lover's silk?

WHEN IN JUNE

Rolling tuscan suckles at the
deep brown breasts of the valley
june is pregnant with her first child
and rumor has it miss marmalade
cast her own star child westbound
two days before (and two days after)
her gold and green locks were set on fire

FAHRENHEIT

As if a satin sheet
Were pulled across the faceless horizon,

As if a lovely face
Were caught by the chance of Her summer spell,

As if an invisible fire
Were hopping from brown shoulder to shoulder...

The heat wave arrived undressed and fashionably late.

BLUE MONOCLE

The flowers are
Crying tears of glass
And Her monocle to
The world this morning is blue.

But, of course,
That's a poet's compromise.

to spring up
is not
seasonal doing

but a reoccurrence
sometimes between the equinoxes
sometimes between the bed sheets

BLACK MARILYN MONROE

I guess
That's the way
You do it to me
Perhaps
You would
Like to kill me
Perhaps
You would
Like to see me gone
The way you
Stopped to let us pass
The way you
And your wife said *Morning*
The way she couldn't
Even look me in the eye
The way she kept
Looking back back back
To check on our progress
It's hysterical really
And you'll be dead
In twenty years' time
And I'll still be writing poetry
In twenty years' time
And by then I suppose
I'll still be wondering why the hell
It's so damn easy for a person to hate
I'm Marilyn Monroe

I have a mole (or something else) on my face

I write
To take
My power
Back
To document
My times
To document
These times
Rolling like
A rolling stone
Slowly swaying left
Never staying too long

I HAD A DREAM

There was the lion
And the bitch
And the portal
Every color you can
Imagine was combining
Every sky you can
Imagine was heading out
It wasn't the apocalypse
Because there wasn't
A title given to the chapter
And it wasn't noisy as one
Would suspect of our ending

It was just a single rose
Expanding east and west

It was quiet
And surprisingly intimate

All thighs no play
All eyes but no falling curtain

STORYTELLER

Wind:
Teach me
Your ways
Of backpacking.

Day:
Teach me
Your ways
Of coloring in.

Night:
Teach me
Your ways
Of storytelling.

EAU DE JOY

I opened a
Bottle of May
But the memory
Was hot to the touch.
The glass shattered
Before I could place
The decanter back
On the counter.

So I cleaned the mess.

SPRING

82 and loving you

When springs says
I love you so much

Like a kiss on the forehead

With His interruptions of
Bloodshot
black-eyed-Susan's

MIMOSA HONEY

Sweet as in pomade
Applied prior to leaving

The bees are jealous
Of the seasons of my curls
And when April is no more
The hive, I know, will begin plotting.

MEMORIAL FLORA

Those fat red miracles
Were among your favorite
But you were not well enough
To care for some of your own.
Had you adopted a rose child
The poor thing would have perished
A very hot and very California death.

You helped everyone
But yourself and when all
Was said and done everyone brought
You just that: over two dozen rose children.

Beauty and the best.

MOMENTARY MONET

Stationary parade

I the buyer prepared my greens and coppers
Carefully she took her
Dawn circles and layered night squares
Out from their five-hour market pedestal.
The feet behind me were careless and nosy
Never had they seen such an arrangement.
How beautiful the wife said
But late July was the mood of the husband.
And so the two of them carried on
But not long after they
Began to walk down this
Alley of citrus and edible gemstones
She and her greying crown of curls
Looked back once more (just to be certain)

Weeks have passed on
And now her Momentary Monet
Has taken to the vintage ways of dying

Slow

    And then even slower

        And then twice as fashionable

But she was right all along.

Flowers, like people, live forever when we
choose to look a little longer

To capture the moment

PRIOR TO STEAMING
THE VEGETABLES

Here is a poem
For the ones who
Have yet to know

It is possible
To place a teabag
In the sky and forget

Yesterday I watched
The evening sky turn from
Dark brown to dark orange

I got really scared
I couldn't figure out why
The day was becoming so

But then I saw
The hanging string
Swinging in the wind

So I
Grabbed it
Quick and went to bed

Not soundly but all right

STORM SYSTEMS

I've collected three versions of this world
But nowhere in these worlds did the wind
Ever not lose ever not stop ever not curl up

And die

FORECASTING

Rain will never know why it happens
It just cries and pouts wherever it wants
And I think that says a lot about how
Some of us ache always or accidentally

Or all at once

THE 3 A. M. GARDENER

There it grows

The spirit of the
Planted has chosen
To persist sideways.

The dream roots tightly.

Nowhere.

MOTHER EARTH

Minuscule green hairs
Dance the tango where
The cracks in the concrete
Have started to look
More like a series of
Connecting constellations
Broke of stars, broke of its own glory,
But familiar with my grandmother's stories.

You see Mother Earth is constantly
At war with Herself and Her creations.
She's so at war that She can't exist without
Having them remind us She is a woman and therefore
marginalized.

The moving image is an
Empty graveyard which is not exactly a graveyard at all
But, metaphorically speaking, the nicest way to
explain how
The Man since the dawn of Our dawn has placed his
interest in faces but not humanity.

These are the hills where grey substance is poured to
make room for the new
But if the tall and the ugly could speak every blade of
grass (I just know) would remain

mute.

We don't deserve an answer but
The grass grows back green anyway

REMEMBERING

There was a girl
You met years ago
Who looked a bit
Like myself
She was Black
She was Brown
She was lovely
She wanted to
Kill herself some days

There was a girl
You met years ago
Standing under the Sun
The Light brought out her Mother's tongue
The Light emphasized all corkscrews and lines
The Light forever immortalized the way she ran
That entire mile in ballet flats
With blisters on her heel and heart

Ready to pop
Ready to burst of flora scented water

Do you remember that girl

I don't
But I do I feel sorry for her for not knowing
better

I don't
But I do

FLOWER STAND ON MISSION

Her arrangements
Are a pretty eyesore
To those in their
Vehicles passing by.

But it was
Also strange
To me.

Just in sight of this
Little slice of
A colorful fake paradise
Sat a group of day walkers;
The ones who make deals with
The Sun more than the Devil himself;
The ones who laugh over bad jokes with
The dandelions in the concrete more than themselves;
The ones who dance like it's Woodstock with
Their feet inching dangerously close to the line of horns.

A slow death is a new hotel built over false love.

IF TODAY WERE
PINK LEMONADE

See me pour
Today in
A tall pitcher

See me
Adding
Some sugar
Watching
The white sink in

See me
Preparing
A glass

Now watch me
Dumping every
Last coral
Colored drop
Over the brown spot in
The front section of the
lawn

SOWING

Beginnings are
Ridden with
Seeds of hope

And my
Fingernails are
Dirty this morning

YOURS IN LEARNING

Sometimes I wonder if metaphors are a curse
Once I use them I forget how good it is to talk straight
And other times I get so dizzy over straightforwardness I
Purposely let myself meditate on nature things altogether

Four leaf clovers that grant bad wishes
And verbena that have overdosed on fertilizer

Lazy rivers
And showers with a patience oh so impressive

But then again there were times I let you align my
words altogether...

I suppose both are working areas for me

GROWTH

Sometimes it will take
Considering that not all
Bouquets have flowers

And other times it will take
Noticing that not
All forms of blossoming

Call for extravagant
Outerwear or the
Harsh light of daytime

PATIENCE

Like a teaspoon
Dipped in honey

Perishable
Until my spoon
Hits the hardwood
And the word is
No longer cracked but laughable

I lost everything
Cause I thought too fast

NOX

They stand there
Watching this
Burning shrinking
Terra cotta hole
In the crazed sangria sky
Dip its ass into the sea.
After exhaling
The Sun quenches
Its array of medallion curls.
But no one claps.
No one's impressed
Because we were born and raised.
And as if those
Old dumbing white caps
Understood law and order
They obey their master
And flee to where rust
For the next twelve hours
Is not the color
Of a bygone memory
But the very hue of perseverance.

UNTITLED

A figure
Of manifestation.
A star
Of loveliness.

That's our autumnal fire(place).

Keep it burning.

SUNRISING

I dip my finger
In the afternoon and
Trace my own sunrising.

Sky ink.
Blue over grey.
The new colors run thin...

But I feel like May today.

SMELLS LIKE FREEDOM

I poured
November
Into a decanter
Earlier this morning.
I wanted to
Save just enough
To spray on a blank page
For a much later recollection or poem.
But the glass cracked straight down the middle.
The jagged shards pretty and light—like strange snow.

What does the longing for freedom and injustice smell
like anyway?

How would they even know?

REVOLUTION

There is revolution
Found in the flower
That grows opposite

BIG BAD PRETTY
FUGLY QUILT

We weave
Halfway quilts
Made of
Halfway metaphors.

Cross-threading
They call it

Then we meet
At the middle
And wonder why.

A luck of the crossroads
They call it

But justice is served
When we switch out
Not the color of the thread
But the spool and the needle.

Until then
You and I
Will remain a
Big bad pretty fugly quilt.

Foxtails are the
Keepers of Promises
And rusting metal fences
With periodic holes are the
Keepers of the Universe

HER STREET OF BIG LITTLE GHOSTS

White hornets
And unloving daddy long legs
And bold butterflies exercising civil disobedience

A cigarette butt flattened by a tire
Then in the middle of the cul-de-sac
There is the ghost of a little girl of
Deep brown skin running across the way
She's Joy
She's the world in one
She's where their smiles have gone to
She's not a ghost but the embodiment of
Some sepia memory from ten years prior
She has yet to know how bright 4:3 her cinema is
And
She has yet to know how the neighbors are critics
And
She has yet to know why words like today and century
Are such an odd way to explain the way we are
constantly passing by old ghosts
Systems

She said

I'm gonna
Write my way out

I'm gonna
Write my way up

I'm gonna
Write my way past Heaven

And then I'm gonna
Set up a lawn chair on Saturn

The child within us all
Lives on regardless if it long ago
Decided to haunt where the days
Were taken in doses rather than half hours.

QUESTION

I've burnt water
Out of old pots

Made the
Bottom blush back black

Does that make me
A bad cook or an overthinker

THE ONE HUNDRED DEGREE DREAM

You are
Everywhere
These days.
I've got
Memories
As high as
November.
But I can't
See autumn
Anymore.

The heat
Has been here
Too long.

THAT HOUSE ON WOULDBOUND STREET

They called them
Easter egg houses
Because the color pallet
Could prove that surprising.
Lavender. Light green. Light blue.

And love was a four o' clock bush with
No flowers leading all the way to the front door.

Sincerity used to be
Placing my lips
Before a wild dandelion.
But it's possible
These old habits
Can revive themselves
In the most unexpected ways.

Talking, too, is to help a mind flower find its way home.

BAD SPIRIT

That's the
way of
a bad spirit

always the
wholesome host
yet never truly wholesome

or there.

IF NOT MARIGOLD

I've seen hope
Take flight from
Grey spaces with
Landings rich in monochrome.

SEPTEMBER

Success is strange
In Southern California.

Where the ground
Isn't already green
It's either in the process
Of turning over or turning dark grey.

Call it a concrete fatality.

POEM FOR M.

A bet made with the unknown is a
bet made with ourselves

I was a
Sky thinker
Thinking of
Becoming a
Sky flyer.

I was a
Sky dreamer
Dreaming up
Horizons of
No return.

Those skies dripped of gold.
Those skies so gold, so full of water.

Tears.

TO TRIP THE WIND
ON A SUMMER'S DAY

You opened your mouth
and took a long sip of
that silver sweetener
their stories said was heaven
you were (possibly) satisfied
with the aftertaste because
the next thing you did
was give yourself to
his grand black comforter
you let the night wash
over your deep brown skin
as if the sensation was
the only good you ever knew
like starting
and resting
and starting up again
the tears blotchy like your

collection of reds and darker reds
and while the memory of us
sitting on the balcony
melting in the sun
does not haunt nor follow me
i suppose your sad legacy serves
as a sort of sour inspiration to me
not in that way but in the sense
that i don't want to end up like you
with my organs functioning separately

seven miracles
seven undoings
seven unhappy propagations

Change is
Seldom yellow
And too much light can
Strike a fever upon the blossoming

That is the lukewarm abyss
Of the early hours of the morning;

And there is no sun in the
Land of two thousand sunrises

THE LAND OF TWO
THOUSAND SUNRISES

Not quite
Loveliness
Not quite
Loneliness
Not quite
Giving up
Not quite anything at all

Not quite
Tomorrow
Not quite
Yesterday
Not quite
Memory
Not quite anything at all

Except the imagination

EARTH POEMS OF COLOR

For we were born children of the sun:

Moving earth poems of warmth and color.

HEAVINESS, LIGHTNESS, SWEETNESS

Father Spring has not cried for a while
And these youngling hills of the valley seem
To have found the humor in what has now been a
Yearlong winter of a monochrome variation of blues.

But that's a moral lesson to be learned another day.

BIG BLUE WONDER

How we share
Big blue wonders
Minding at all
Minding our own
Minding for a moment
Without cracking
For the better or worse
Is beyond my will to wonder.

Maybe, in heaven,
There are no clashing symphonies.

Maybe, in heaven,
There are no cackling gulls of white.

The to-be-plucked (Asian pears)
Were in desperate need of attention
And the little baby blue bird that lost
Its soaring spirit was anything but
A revolution in the making
But it, like us, like everyone
Allowed itself to believe life was
Truly worth living and managed to fly to
Someplace, somewhere, where
Its night immediately became Hell or Heaven
The weather, too, was a raging symphony
It arrived uninvited and it carried us on its shoulder
But when the Night inherited Her glowing crown
The streets were swaying a familiar R&B song

pop!

pop!
pop!

It was their light show of sparkling champagne
(without the alcohol)
The charcoal hating to even mix—
Like that one time ten decades ago
Thirty minutes had passed us by
When the fireworks raised a white flag

And then, out of nowhere, at 1 p.m.,
The agony revived itself gloriously
Everyone was asleep by then but I was still awake
Thinking about my (our) funny state of being

Here we were
Americans
Shouting prose
Louder than car horns
Thinking
This was exactly
What it means
To be free as the wind

To be free as an American
Through
The stubborn eye
And the biased eye
And the unwilling eye
The blood of the past will run not dark or bright red

But grey

FEELS LIKE

Freedom
Can't even
Afford itself
Freedom
Can't even
Fit inside itself
Because freedom
Isn't spacious.

It's small.

Inside.

THE GOOD ONES

I'm not proposing
We share the water

I'm asking you to
Set your fire out

So we can get
A new fire going

"Gently...gently..."
Her voice echoes in my mind.
"Cast gently into the wind."

II

VER

BE

NA

THREAD COUNT

Little girl got her jumpers dirty
Her dresses had
Big and small holes in them
And these holes which
Were later stitched back together
By her mother
Who always used the same box
But never a brighter shade of thread was
All a metaphor to the greater things in life

INDIGO MOUNTAIN OCEAN MIRACLE

Suppose that wonder of
Synthetic lemon was dyed
Dark yellow for visibility's sake.
Would the scent still remind you
Of California's first-born child
Like it did me when I sprayed it?

Maybe one day
The entire coastline
Will be laid to rest forever.
Maybe you and I
Will finally learn how to
Live and love with the remainder.

Or maybe we won't learn anything at all.

ON THE DAY EARTH CRIES SAFFRON

If this is the way
The world will end
The conversations
Too light
Too dark
Too strange
Too much (of that)
And the shorelines
Too blue
Too invading
Too late
Too late
I don't think I'll
Ever get tired of
Writing about how
Ironic it is we look to
The skies harboring
No expectations
And yet
Every longing imaginable

On the day the Earth cries
Saffron you and I will be there

Nevertheless

How much Earth
We take is
How much Earth
We've already forbidden from ourselves

GIRL GONE

Young girl walks
Into a Walmart with
Her grandmother
Who is Black and wonderful.

The cashier says
Is that your daughter
And the grandmother smiles proudly
She says
No that's my granddaughter
And the cashier kind of smiles too
She says
It'd be a shame if someone took her
And that's when politeness left quicker than a paycheck
The grandmother says
What do you mean
And the cashier she just says
She has that look some people like

She looks like everybody

Aunt
And
Grandmother
And
Daughter
And
Mother
Standing together
In a too small of a bathroom
Teaching each other
The way of the braid
The way of oil and hot and cold water.
"Like this," someone says. "You gotta make sure—"
But the exact words, like her passed-down scrunchies,
have lost me now.

Aunt
And
Grandmother
And
Daughter
And
Mother
Standing together
In a too small of a bathroom
Not noticing (except for the daughter)
How cold the draft coming in from the open window is.

The early spring air
The mixing of flora and chemical flora.
"And see Marilyn, if you comb her hair out with
your fingers—"
But the exact words, again, are nothing more than a
face expression today.

Pink's Luster.
Just For Me.
Hair Food (in the clear jar).
Some orange or bright green tube of vitamins E and A.
The wood comb with a glistening wood handle.

The warm light from above being turned on, and then
off, is something of God.

NOW KNOWS NO CLOCK

Organic rising.
Green but without the pesticides.
Not a single one-size-fits-all pot.

My herb beds are
A mess but isn't that how
It's supposed to be on some days?

ASIAN MARKET ON MISSION

Pito Pito
Sambong
Ampalaya

Little red box
Sitting next to a
Brown mortar gifted

From my mother
Sitting next to a
Packet of dried seaweed

And ginger
And astragalus
And black seed oil capsules

All but two
From the local Asian market
Where eight-year-old me snitched

On a man
For stealing shrimp
From the kitchen located in the back

They fried fish there
They sold fresh tilapia and mussels
And to this day the hot oil pops the same

BLACKTOP CHRONICLE

But i still remember that girl playing tetherball
turning her skin purple and her knuckles banged up
before first period has even begun all because this boy
who said he could beat her because he's much stronger
had a convincing smile and a convincing way
of persuading.

Neither of us knew it then
and maybe i still don't know
but it was as if the game itself
would forecast the next thirty years.

I didn't win
and
i didn't walk away dry
but i still remember that girl coming in rough,
coming in with her training bra showing.

TO BE A WRITER IS NOT A COMING
OR A NOTICING BUT A SIT DOWN

The question was
When do we discover we are artists?

But to tell the truth I still don't think
There's a place or time for an answer.
One way of putting it is
How many times did we
Know freedom like we did
Know relief like we did
When we did our thing (when no one else knew)
When our hands were busy doing all of those things.

For example:

When I was in school I was
Sitting in Literature class when
A teacher who was Black came in quietly.
Her bag was brown and her hair was curly and styled
short like my Auntie Lisa's.
She called each of us one by one to the corner where
we were tasked to write about
Anything and for whatever she found was necessary
(or required) for her to study us.
I don't recall what I wrote but I remember how my
hands moved and how she asked

"Do you write at home?" followed by "You write what comes to your mind, don't you?"
As if she knew something I didn't or thought something I simply couldn't think unless I was her.

To this day I still don't know why she was there (I wasn't paying attention).
All I know is that when the bell rang I left as if someone important was actually waiting for me.

IDENTITY

Lingering eyes
Can strike a kill
Better than
Moving mouths
Ever could

Notice how
It's almost always
The watchers that
Mistake song birds for cats

Never cats for beautiful song birds

A NOTICING

When they
Tell you
What they aren't

When they
Show you
What they are

Notice not
Their words but
Their lack of hesitation

WALKING

Feels like
I'm following
A diamond
Come here
Baby nigga
Come over
Come over
Come over
HERE
Baby nigga
You're so beautiful
You're so beautiful
Did you hear what I said
I said did you hear what I said
I said you're beautiful girl
I said you're beautiful girl
Wait you're mixed right
So you're BLACK mixed with WHAT

SIS MAGNOLIA

On the day
I see that tree
Give all she can
Just for me
I swear I will
Propagate one
Of her branches
Just so she can
Start and bloom all over again
And know love for herself
And bathe in the July Sun
And trade stories with the honeybees
And realize even though it's a strange living to be a woman
It can also be a pretty colorful and joyous one too

SOMEBODY SHOT A CANARY

Days I have
Absolutely nothing
To say aloud or to you

Because
                    ...it's like...
We're
Always talking about change
Always talking about changing
Always talking about shedding our skin
But then something, somewhere, happens.

There's nothing poetic about the happening.
Maybe there's something to pull out from there
But you can't carry a casket on the back of a poem.

You can only carry the times and their name(s).

THE CROW WON'T LEAVE, WON'T BUDGE, WON'T WEEP

Fallen crows
Turn into
Rubble
Turn into
Materials
Turn into
Wider institutions
Turn old
Blazers into new
Turn old
Smiles into nervous smiles
Turn wrinkled
Hands into softer hands
Which hold
Double-headed pens
Which sign
Double-sided city skylines

A BLACK GIRL WALKS INTO A CAFÉ

I enter this small cafe
And when I sit down it
Does not go unnoticed that
It took only thirty seconds
For at least ten pairs of eyes to
Take notice of my lack of lacking
I'm standing here at the front because
I don't know where the hell he's sitting
He didn't tell me what he was wearing
Nor did he care to let me know he's the one
Sitting by the window wearing a dark grey hoodie (fuck!)
With his head blocked by the dark square of his silent
flickering machine

So I sit down and she, a white dove,
No less than ten seconds
After I place my folder and documents on the table
Gets on up like James Brown

The remaining stares carry on like waterfalls
Heavy on my back and on my sides and my head
It's like you're suffocating but you're more than capable

He just said something mixed with do you have a copy
of your social
But I missed the first half because I'm letting my
anxiety get the best of me today

And these people are still watching
And he's joking about how he didn't know if it was
really me

As if I'm not the only one here
With nostrils
Like this
With skin
Like this
With hair
Like this
With dreams so Black so Brown
Like this

MARCH 16

Mother tell me
Where the end
Of the rainbow is
Where the roads
Of our town smile back
Where the word
Brown or Black is not
A face
Or
Another part of the story
Or
Another part of the headline
Or
Another part of the article which states
"They appear to be female and Asian."

If rainbows
Have endings
The ending is not there or anywhere out there.

Maybe the ending is within us

STRANGERS

If I hold
My breath
Long enough
Will you
Tell me it's
Not ok to not be ok
Or will you
Tell me it also matters
If my surname strikes you as familiar?

We look the opposite way
Much like the winter does fall:
Carelessly yet naturally yet
Nevertheless nothing less than human.

I release
My breath
For me

FOR A COUSIN, FOR A FRIEND

Asking for a friend
Who is dead
Who is Black
Who is Brown
Who was their mother
Who was their father
Who was their childhood friend
Who knew everybody but nobody
Who was not a friend of mine
But a cousin by way of the headlines.

Have the times spoken?
Or have we, the people, spoken over the other?

AND I'LL REMIND YOU HOW HE DIED

Tell me where
The times have changed
Where the blues
Are not blue
Where the reds
Are not red stains.

HAND ME A FLOWER AND
I'LL HAND YOU THE BLUES*

Hand me a flower
And I'll hand you the blues.
Hand me a flower
And I'll tell you the story of
How my grandmother's brother
Was killed by the KKK after
Word spread that our family discovered oil on our farm;
How a man by the name of Private Charles Lewis
Who, in 1940, was lynched in Kentucky after refusing
To empty pockets while wearing his Army uniform.

Hand me a flower and
I'll hand you the blues.
Hand me a flower
And I'll return you an entire century of
The weight of the Black bodies, like Will Brown,
Who was beaten and hanged from a telegraph post
All before his body was dragged through the street;
The sound of an entire town called Rosewood which,
in 1923,
Was gutted out and burned to the ground by White
mobs after

* *Originally written for KNOCK LA in collaboration with photographer Caroline Johnson for the part poetry, part photo essay project (The Noise This Evening) which covered the summer LA protests of 2020**

A man named Jesse Hunter was framed for assaulting
a White woman.
Hand me a flower
And I'll tell you this.
Hand me a flower
And I'll tell you this without flinching:

ISLANDS

I remember what
She said to me then
She said when she came
She learned our silver and copper
She learned what it means to love a Black woman
She learned how to start with nothing yet everything
She learned it's actually rather dangerous to drive with
both feet

And here I am—wondering why I am so unsure when
I was born with the longer stick

When they say America has come a long way
They really mean the American people have walked
another inch

FOUR BORDERS, WRITTEN IN SHARPIE:
WELCOME TO THE REVOLUTION[†]

Should we die
Should we ever die
So loud and so softly
Should we cry
Should we ever cry out
For our mothers
Who will proclaim
Jim Crow had a Grandchild?
Who will know the color blue as we've known it?

When we're done marching
When we're back safe and home for the night
Who will know the dying living lie that is America?
Who will say it?
Will somebody say it?
Should we sleep so loud and so softly
Who will know so many years from now
That when we said his name and His name
These streets were red and aglow with a new
hallelujah?

† *Originally written for KNOCK LA in collaboration with photogra-*
pher Caroline Johnson for the part poetry, part photo essay project (The
*Noise This Evening) which covered the summer LA protests of 2020**

Revolution now.
Revolution now.

Revolution (inhale, exhale).
Revolution (inhale, exhale).

Revolution now.
Revolution now.

Revolution (inhale, exhale).
Revolution (inhale, exhale).

For to know
AMERICA
And to strike
AMERICA
Through Her ribs
One must breathe
AMERICA
Like
AMERICA
Is both the oxygen and the culprit of all suffocation
Like to win
AMERICA over one must walk to the pace of
AMERICA 24/7.

‡   *Originally written for KNOCK LA in collaboration with photogra-
pher Caroline Johnson for the part poetry, part photo essay project (The
Noise This Evening) which covered the summer LA protests of 2020**

Revolution now.
Revolution now.

Revolution (inhale, exhale)
Revolution (inhale, exhale).

Revolution now.
Revolution now.

Revolution (inhale, exhale)
Revolution (inhale, exhale).

WOMAN SHE, WOMAN WHO

I am a woman
So you
Treat me
Like a woman
Talk to me
Like a woman
Hit me up
Like a woman
So bad so discreetly
You could be woman too.

It can only take something
Of divine intervention
They say
For something
So divine and so tragic to find residency
In the eyes of those who saw it all and all at once.

It can only take something
So wicked and so depressing
They say
For this many screens and this many people
To get out from the flickering darkness of their homes
With no other intention but to become it, to know it
for themselves.

The revolution was already here.
The revolution was already rooted.

So why not blame divine intervention
For the world finally getting off its butt to march for
justice first color second?

They say
All this
And I'm thinking
Loud and saying nothing

§ *Originally written for KNOCK LA in collaboration with photographer Caroline Johnson for the part poetry, part photo essay project (The Noise This Evening) which covered the summer LA protests of 2020**

MIDDLE

Spare me from
Your seeking eye
Your lazy arrows
Your gaping bias
We are only
Skeleton after all
Walking marrow
Walking tall
To be buried next
To the willow tree
The tree made
Famous by BH
Who once sang that
Haunting song of
Fruiting trees with
No fruit no bees.

Know me? No. Try again.

I'm the trickiest moving target.

I'm the bull's eye made of
Asian vine and African jade and American pearls.

As if
WOMAN
Or
WOMAN OF COLOR
Are really that scary of
Words upon being capitalized

BEHOLD THE UNPROMISED LAND

These images of
Sea and land
Sea meeting land
Call to me
But there is always
The sail of these
Old cranky ships
Sailing wearily
Under the tar sun
Which drips tar sundrops.

I want to meet you
But I can only go back so far
And even then it's like
Would you even recognize me?

Would you see more of her than him?

KANSAS CITY GIRL

One day you're sitting
In History class with a close friend
Who proceeds to tell you the obvious
And then next day she's gone and possibly pregnant
with her first

You're both in your twenties now but the memory
smells pungent

She said *You would've been my slave*
She said this with a pretty blonde girl smile
She said this as you were looking down at
These grey faces with grey smiles who were
Smiling over the swaying of the corpse of course
The smoke is
Curling like a ribbon
The mood is
A burning desire to travel backwards in time and tell
her how it is

But you didn't say anything
You didn't say anything because
You were caught up in this assumption
That maybe it was
A finger
A leg
An ear
They cut off
To take home to their spouses and hellhounds

THE LAND OF RED SOIL AND ROSES

Sea of
White and power
To burn you
Out of existence
Would be too easy

OIL

From behind
The vehicle
Coughed
Pushed on like
Some hellish chariot.
The time it took
Is lost to my ears
Because I didn't ask.
But that was the word: oil.

Louisiana to Arkansas.
He passed on
The day of the crash
And she
Never told me this herself
But she
Once said to me
When I was much younger that
One of her father's favorite sayings
Was, *When there is a will, there is a way.*

WE ARE ALL BORN GREEN (2052)

We will either
Peel our globe
Like the skin
Of a tangerine
Slowly
Gradually
Never all the way together
Or we will burn
The green and the brown
Like they did
Sugarcane stalks
Slowly
Gradually
Never all the way together

NEW NORMAL

Lines occupy the
Sides of her beige face
After wearing her mask
For so long so damn long
And this boy who is far from
Being a boy but not wise enough
To be called a man asks his friend
As they're riding their bikes up the strand if
He was the one who drank his drink without asking.

Time will be the author of our reddening novel.

MY GRANDMOTHER'S CHARIOT

It goes a little
Something like this
A little bit of heaven
A little bit of her fiery chariot
Exits from your mouth each time
You speak and because the receiver
Is not a woman, is not knowledgeable of
The power of guavas or the little ways such
Drafts can still perfume a person twenty years after
The silence is taken as a product of unannounced storms
As opposed to a natural occurrence of a natural soft-
ness and a natural perseverance.

ONE LINE HIGHLIGHTED BOLD

We're not together
But stuck like super glue
Sewn into the same blue and white and red flag
For the better or the worse or the worse of two evils.

Blood is running on the concrete—but whose is it?

Has the other side noticed or learned?

OF DUSK AND GHOSTS AND IRONY

I'm violet
All over
All afternoon

COLORISM

You said
You are my
Goldilocks.

Not too curly.
Not too light.
Not too dark.

You said
You are my
Medallion warbler.

But to tell the truth
I want to kill myself
Sometimes over your ivory eye.

To hell with your privileged perch.

MYSELF

Because it
Seems you've
Already met me
Already know my architecture
Already hot waxed my surname
from first letter to last...

Sometimes I just lose myself thinking
about the possibilities.

IMAGINE THAT

The stars sighing
Just for the heck of it

The storm clouds dressing
The moon up in Valentino

The town flipping
Upside down as she

Breaks free from the
Should have tree the

Tree of her
Mother's root

PARDON

if i speak
in all capital letters
will you hear me
or hear me a little better?

when i raise my voice
i see you lean in
as if that will unleash
all of what is contained
inside this little gold box inside me.

I SAID
IT'S
NICE TO
MEET YOU.

I SAID
LET ME
MEET YOU
AS I AM.

THE BIRD OF PARADISE SET FREE

Little fires burning inside
Little footsteps as I proceed down the stairs.

Another glory bird cries out—but the key and the cage
have wed.

THE HAND: THE CUP,
THE SPOON, THE SPRINKLER

Added that to
Her cast iron
Along with
One large egg
A cup of flour
A cup of cornmeal
A cup of whole milk
And a cup of some
Distant warm nightbreak.

It was always Southern-style cornbread.

Always a little sweet.

Wind
Was
Spirit
Was
Lost
Memoir

MOTHER'S TONGUE

In a language
I hear yet don't recall
The words tease me
Make a knot of my tongue
Cause my gums to bleed out.

I butcher the
Word and try again.

Now I've got it.
Now I've lost it—again.

Still you say
I'm your guava girl.

APU'S PLACE

Chances come and go
Like kalamansi
Calling out to be picked or rotting on the ground

DADDY LONG-LEGS BLUES

Past the rectangular frame
of the door of her house sat
a queen-sized bed that was occupied
by no queens and no kings but instead
these eight-legged creatures that had
hearts smaller than a grain of salt and
eyes with vortexes bigger than sedona in arizona
the dust, the '70s, moving in and out in real time

THE TIMES COME AND GO BUT
WE WILL ALWAYS BE THE TIMES

Learning the ways
Of which they say
Are learned at least
Three different times
Through the eyes of
Three different women
Living in the times of
Three different uprisings

GRANNY'S HOUSE

She called it
Treasure hunting
The way I would
Run up and down
The green shaggy carpet with
Something old
Something Avon in my hand

SEEKING

Grey faces
Sit at a table
But provide
No answer.

Is it too late
To know more
Because you've
Gone Home?

Have I been
Asking questions
From the wrong chair?

GRACIE LEE OSBORNE

Ebony strong.
A firm softness
Just like her name: Grace.

You're
1936
Sagittarius
Without
Having to
Prove it
Without
Having to
Buy a necklace
To explain that's your sign
Jonesboro
Louisiana
Eyes
So pretty
So deep brown
The laugh
The warmth capable
Of making even the stubbornest river
Curve into something of a silly smile
You're
1936
Sagittarius
Without Having to
Say it

Without
Having to
Tap on my shoulder from Heaven

TUESDAY KITCHEN TABLE DIARY

She sat in a chair
Feet up on the cushion
Knees before the kitchen table
She was eating KFC chicken with
An elder who was explaining
What it was like
To do that one thing
Back in the day
Like no one else could
Like no one but String Bean could
She ran all that way
She ran so fast the crowd gave her a nickname
But see she's
A hardheaded girl
A girl listening in half frequencies

Thus the titled poem remains highly uncertain

Unchecked

Now all of the
Angels and clouds of
Heaven come to her door just
So they can say they sat over her cooking too.

DOTAGE

They sat there lined up like ducks
Listening to this woman sing a song
Made for children as if they were children too.

Time is not an answer it is a compromise
between now and when

NORTH OF NORTH RIVER ROAD

Pendleton where have you gone
I can see your peaks but it's the
Green of your back that's lost me.

They're building houses on your heart
They're digging up your veins and your marrow
But you do not cry do not make noise instead
You send Mother Coyote and the spirits of her
Four children down to the riverbed at San Luis Rey
To recite that God awful poetry at what better time
than 3 a. m.

THE BEGINNING

Bright light.
The birth of Day.
The birth of Umbra.
The birth of mourning.
The birth of the black bird, Black heartbeat.

Then, like a pan does when one adds too much oil,
Everything began to pop, to crackle, to spill out, to
talk its way
Out of the skillet that is The Universe and all of the
ugly pretty things within it.

This is how far we go back.

It starts with an eye or maybe a star.

REVELATIONS

We were wedding crashers. Spring and winter were
getting married. But She changed her mind at the last
minute. Threw the ring off to the side and asked her
emerald bridesmaids to help her set the whole meadow
on fire. Winter promised to change. He promised to
be a fireplace from then on but how can the King of
white and standstill possibly commit to ridding such
old habits? The flames, rising, building, was light like
lavender and from a distance I could hear the sound of
a Woman better known as your local metropolis crash-
ing in on Herself.

Then the trumpets started and jazz was born again.

PRAYER

Lord I think
I want to kill myself

Lord I think
I want to wring out the night

But I'm going
To try Lord

I'm going
To get better Lord

I'm going
To write a pretty poem now

SONG FOR CHYNA

Honeysuckle dreams
Don't mean the same
Don't talk to me
Now that August is over

You take the night
You take the call
You call him bad
And then you

Fall

Chyna
Hanging from the tree
Hanging from the wall
The day is done, the Sun is tall

You take the night
You take the call
You call him bad
And then you

Call me

Summertime
Is the time
For picking cherries

So pretty, so red
But August is over

Honeysuckle dreams
Don't mean the same
Don't talk to me
Now that you don't

Call me

STATIC

Childhood friend
I think I thought
Of you this morning

I saw your face in
Someone else today
And now that I'm stuck guessing

I can't help
But wonder who
Exactly left first

And if fruit flies
Can cause trouble
In floating lands of cloud and sky water

And if the sound
Of those old songs our parents loved truly
Change their tune once they reach Saint Peter's gate

THE BLUE MIDNIGHT SUN

It came to me in a dream. There was The Fog and the ruins of some place the other one claimed was abandoned for reasons related to politics. The mist moved its long grey fingertips up and around my body and around the edge of the mountain ridge that was monochrome like the rest of it. I was under the spell of this world without primary color, but in the end it turned out none of it was mine to keep. When I tried to claim it upon waking I lost everything immediately. Then, one day, I saw the blue midnight sun. I saw something of fantasy there and I tried to flesh it out. I tried to charm the story back to me but it proved to be stubborn. Now I'm making my way one night, one dream at a time.

SUMMER OF FLEA

This lady who owned
Seventeen cats had seventeen
Colonies of fleas to give a fuck about
They didn't have names (I don't think)
All she had to say was "Here, kitty kitty!"
And they would come running across the way like that
But during that summer
Of itching
Of smells
Of rotting flesh
One cat did not come when
My grandmother who was cat sitting called out into
the hall

It was white all over and was laying underneath
The family's old red pick-up truck in the garage
I was the one who discovered it first and I was so terrified
And I don't remember if there was hesitation but there was
A sort of quickness that was present throughout the
whole ordeal
She didn't want me to know its body geometry but it
was too late

At least to memory there was
No grave
No ceremony
No crying for this poor dead cat
There was only the disturbed and the disappointed

To this day I itch at the thought of sitting in that
plastic chair on the front porch
Reading children's books from the local library until I
was done and curious again

MUST WE LEAVE WITH UNFINISHED BUSINESS?

All the beasts
Stretch their arms
Out and apart
And to the same place

All the people
Stretch their arms
Out and apart
And to the same place

CHAPEL HILL

These stones
I know too well
I've read their names
And I know where the
Mr. and Mrs. lay forever
And I know where the
Ground likes to perk up
Between the months of
March and May but I
Don't know them
Don't care to wonder further
Because if I do I may scare myself
Just like I did when I was eight or so.

Back then I believed skeletons could
Get up and get down like they did in *Thriller*.

*Speaking up is not the same
as speaking violet in the rain.*

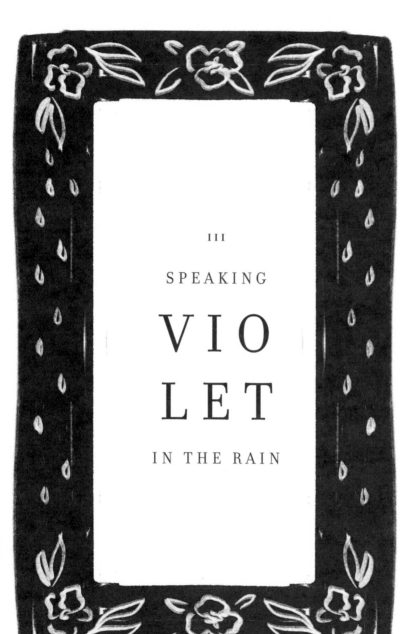

III

SPEAKING

VIO
LET

IN THE RAIN

COMBUSTION

I rushed myself
As if my very life
Depended on it

And now that
I've crossed that
Invisible finish line

I've realized there
Is a fire within us all
That will either

Keep us warm or kill us
From the inside out
If we let it have its way

JUST THE LEMON

But it wasn't
As easy as
Cutting a lemon
And squeezing
Every last bit of
Unlucky out from it.
You can make
Something sweet
With sugar but
You can't kill sour
And certainly
You can't kill
Fallen seeds either.

The sting
Just floats
In the cup
Until a spoon or a finger
(Or a poem) gives it mercy.

WHY?

And you said that
As if aiming my arrow
At the lazy eye of tomorrow
Is the equivalent to sin

If something spills
After I hit my target
The cleanup is on me
And I'm perfectly fine with that

SOULFIRE

Trying mindfully is
Not the same as trying
Until gravity decides for us

ODE TO SYLVIA'S STAR

Call me stubborn
But if you knock down
The Big and Little Dipper while
Trying to extend
Your hand past the Moon
I wouldn't mind rehoming them

At my place

MERCY, MERCY, MERCY

If I break a
Bone and keep
Walking does
That mean I'm
Stubborn?

If I break

All

The way

Down

And keep
Walking
Does that
Mean I'm
Human?

If I break up
My lines too
Quickly does
That mean I'm
A sneezing poet?

THE ROAD IS LONG AND
LONELY AND PAVED BLACK

I walked
The Earth
While lying in bed.
Back against the duvet
I walked to some flattery
That wasn't
Entirely there nor
Entirely familiar to yours or mine

Indeed it was
A happy place
With happy paintings
(Impressionism was the honeybee's forte)
And of course
After I looked back
I eventually walked on without hesitation

I was on my way
I was a beautiful canary
Unaware roads are more than capable of
having personalities

TELEPATHY

Little land mines
Buried beneath
Cherry blossom trees
Land of no flaw
Land of no sea
Look around you
Look around you
Look around you
Perfect is not
A place or a dream
It is a vortex leading
To a never-was-star

I can't tell you
To appreciate you
Because appreciating yourself
Isn't the same as appreciating myself
But I should have
You know these scars
On my body were never
Something to slip off something to toss away like
An old raincoat I didn't need in the first place or
A broken terra cotta pot that shouldn't have been
placed there

I'm stuck

With what
I've got
And now
I can tell
Stories
Without
Moving my lips

BE SOFT, BE SOFT

But
Would you
Be mean to that
Little face in the mirror
Would you
Be bad to that
Twisted up face in the Polaroid
The one they could never get to behave
The one they could never get to smile big
The one they could never get to stand still
Because they had somewhere to be
Because they knew how strange it is to ask a person
To smile or to say cheese when they don't mean it?

Would you
Tell that little girl that little boy

To never go for it
To never daydream
To shut the fuck up
To never speak on it
To never take a second glance
To never take the extra time
When they need the extra time?

I scratched
My way into myself
Not because
I was fed up
But because I was fed up
And believed
I looked like
Someone who deserved it.

She said patience is
A pot of boiling water
Poured at the trunk of a burning
Two-hundred-year-old willow tree

HOW FAR WE MAKE IT (2050)

Now if I snatch
The Moon I'll
Bring down
The whole damn Sky.

And if you kidnap
The Sky you'll cause
The dreamers to admire deep holes.

How about we
Meet in
The middle
And bring the world together with poetry?

How about we
Meet somewhere
Halfway
And plot green architecture (for a greener future?)

The Earth
Is
Already dying.

And we
Are
Already dying.

And love the
Two of us have
Already shouted monopoly

As loud
As our
Shriveling lungs can stand it.

So why
The hell
Not?

How about we
Collaborate
Just so we can see?

HOPE

I carry a
Single seed
Of hope to
Plant possibly

Never

THAT NOBODY KNOWS WHY

With all this talk of
Flowers wise enough
To know it's best not to
Offer advice to the grieving…

With all this talk of
Forever blue skies
Harboring not a single idea
Of moving on in a single day…

With all this talk of
The babied ones and the bees
Gathering their morals to
Survive the coming white winter…

You'd
Think
You and I
Would have known by now

RAYBEARER

You gave
And
You gave
And your handle
Nearly killed
This little sunflower

GREENHOUSE

I am
A greenhouse
Admire me
As you will
Critique me
Over my lack of
Timely blossoming
But I will
Live for years to come
Look at my mind flowers
You can't spray
Pesticides on the written word
You can't kill
What grows black
Or
What grows beyond the ivory line

HONEYDEW

How much
I fail to load
Into my fridge is
Not as important as
How much of the
Fruit you gifted me
Was peeled to hide the mold

THE FOREST OF EAGER

There
Will be an
Impressive
Bull or
Lion or
Swarm
To chase me
Should I find
Myself walking
Past the gates of
The Forest of Eager.

The footprints of
The beasts there have no sound.
And those green Pothos vines which
Hang in a lazy way from high above
Will not warn me should my back position
Opposite of one of the previously mentioned.

No.
No.
There will
Be no
Bull or
Lion or
Swarm.

There will
Only be
The truth and
The start and
The toss-of-the-dice ending.

Unless I can help the feeling

TO MOVE IS NOT AN ACT
OF FORWARDING BUT TURNING

Unlearning
Can burn
Can loosen
Can terminate
Can also be
A sunflower
Looking down
At its scorched petals
And choosing
Not to follow the sun

THE CHILD OF MIDNIGHT

The emphasis
It seems is forever
Badged onto the night
It's natural to assume
My greatest hardships
Occurred in dark rooms
But the truth is that
I'm still one of those people
Who allow twelve o' clock
To sit on my back like a baby
During the middle of the day
There are days I just don't know why
And
There are days I tell you I'm doing fine
And
There are days I answer with *Nothing* when
You ask *Are you all right* or *Do you need to talk*

But it's nothing personal

I'm still learning how to get rid of this child
I did not birth, did not name, did not find loveliness in
its eyes

TO BE STICKY ALL OVER
WITH SWEET SUMMERTIME KISSES

There was
Only so
Much story
I could
Harbor before
I gave
Like February.
My storms
Were caged
Chameleons
Exposed to
No other season but winter.
And when I bled I bled black
Because I was that wed to midnight.

Now the
Seasons
Have changed.
Winter has turned to spring
And north finally looks more
Like a canvas and less like a destination.

But on some days, still, I wonder how many faces I missed.

UNSPOKEN

You talk
About
Milking
Sunshine
From
A cow with no corners
Cashing out love
From
A memory with not a single light source
And it
Makes me
Wonder sometimes
It really
Makes me
Wonder when I hear you say it
Because I've never heard of a person revisiting
A trouble that has troubled them for too long without
Leaving with at least a single sign they broke a sweat
in the process.

Tell me.

Do you want to know my story
Or are you looking to say something pretty
The moment after I've stopped blabbing about my
basket and the yew tree in the backyard?

SECOND TIME'S A CHARM,
THIRD TIME'S A WEEPER

It wasn't
A question of
How many flowers
It took to stink up
A room but how long
It took for you to realize just as
The dead don't acknowledge the living
The lost don't cry for the found or the heartbroken.

DREAMING

Like holding
My breath in
The middle of
Longing or imagining
The heavens dividing in two;
The pieces falling like strange snow
Soft and translucent and dandelion-like
Fluttering
            And landing
                    Nowhere yet everywhere.

Even on my hair.
Even on my black lockbox of California dreams.

NORMALCY

One of these
Days you're going to see
Me wearing a brand new bohemian dress.
Maybe orange. Maybe beige. Maybe floral.

One of these
Days you're going to see
Me wearing something other than honey quartz.
Maybe pure gold. Maybe silver. Maybe moonstone.

One of these
Days we're going
To be dancing our way to each other
Laughing it up so loud and so bad and so tall like it's
New Year's Eve.

We're going to be having
Such a good time we're going
To forget, just for a moment, there was
Ever such a time the lower half of our faces were no
more sporadic than Heaven.

FLICKER IN THE SKY

Shooting stars
Are tired of me
Wishing on them

Shooting stars
Are tired of me
Telling them my shit

And shooting stars
Don't want to be
Shooting stars

And what exactly
Do shooting stars wish on anyway
Do they wish on themselves or do they let themselves

Drop

Drop

Drop

Until grounding is suddenly a matter of meeting?

CHANCE

How
Many times
Am I
Gonna throw
The key off to
The side after
I've headed
Out the door

Look at
Me pretending like
I don't know I'm the only chance I've got

How
Many times
Are you
Gonna press
The entire year against
My brown cheek before
I've looked
Into the mirror

Look at
Me acting like
I don't know I'm pretty

How
Many ways
Are you

Gonna tell yourself
I don't love myself
I don't love myself
I don't love myself
I don't love myself

Look at
You looking at me
Trying to convince me two unwanted rights make a right

ON OUR WAY

There is
The taker
And
The chooser
And there is
The gold stamp
And
The heavy envelope.

The point
Is that neither
Were addressed
To you or to me.

DREAMING

Maybe you and I
Are already filled with bright white fluff;
The night skies we told our black heart secrets to.

Maybe you and I
Are already indifferent on that:
Manifestations leading to hard work leading to reality.

But do you remember
That face
So ready so ready so ready
To challenge the highest of contraries?

Is it
No longer
Enough to levitate
Just for the fun of it all?

Love when was
The last time
You allowed yourself to f l y
Just to see where these smoke-filled borders will allow
you to travel?

We were
On our way
And springing
On our own time

TO HAPPY A TRYING FLOWER

But there's
No room for
Metaphor
No room for
Pretty or
Half awake
Flowers
When the topic
Of the hour is death.

Maybe there's
A frame to hang the
Bigger picture:
Thorny stems that
Are rather unkind
Are rather amusing (in that way).

But I'm
Here now.
I'm so
Here and
I'm so
Done with
You acting
Acting as if
The solution to
The problem

The crack
The demon in the corner of the room
Is the same solution to
The poet's tribulation when they're
Busy making ink liquor for you and I to drink.

You're selling me
Sunflowers but
I have no change.

So where
Exactly did
That black dot go?

WORDS FOR THE WEARY

It's not
Entirely impossible
Or
Uncanny
Or
Uncommon
To take out
Our own reflection
Without staining
The bathroom floor red

Don't be kind to yourself; be honorable

THE WATER MOCCASIN BEACHES ITSELF

When my sky cherries and green perceptions have failed me, I can assure you I will let myself cry a God-awful ocean. Because that's what he asked me that morning: "Are you gonna do it?" And for not knowing it's simply wrong for a person to hold on, to become a bottle, I forced my blues to stay until they could no longer stand my body. As punishment, my heart drowned itself, so I would have no choice but to rescue it.

Now, the times are poppy-minded again.

ALL YOU NEED IS YOU

But love you
Don't have
To be
Golden
Or
Prepared
Or
Rich with intricate literature
Or
Dressed from head to toe in the times

Being
Is
Enough
And
Persevering
Is
An intimate kind of paving
And
Love
We are
Already here.

SPEAKING VIOLETS IN THE RAIN

Some
Take their time
And some
Take it all
But I've always
Found it admirable
How some are able
To befriend the middle
And trip
And not mind the mess
And take their time getting up
And still speak violets in the rain.

That indigo wisdom.

THE SUN CRIES MARY

If these are
Times for winning
Then I will step
Slowly
Slowly
Slowly
Into your fawning ultraviolent

IF THAT WAS HAPPINESS

They say
Steadying
Is possibly
The same as
Stilling
But if it were
That easy
And
That wonderful
Don't you think
Each
And
Every one of us would
Have passed out already?

Sitting so
Long made
The curtains sweat
They were
So tired of watching me.

EACH DAY

Has its
Knots
And
Flyaways

Has its
Bends
And
Straightaways

Has its
Overused
And
Undiscovered leeways

MAKING WAY

Temporarily speaking
I'm water and bone
Indefinitely speaking
I'm a voice in the dusk

Together you and I
Are the wandering and the to-be-wandered
The who and the when
The blank star and the gathering black center

It's not a matter of fantasy but the irony of being prompted to wonder—and to wonder again—despite it all.

IV

THE BLUE

MID
NI
GHT

SUN

AMARYLLIS

I guess it
Was only
Natural I
Never clicked
With stories of
High castles
And
Fancy dresses
And
Long hair
And
Sitting women
When I
Was younger
I wrote
Long and short stories about
Aliens
And shooting stars
And flat flying disks with no windows
There were no
Men or women
There were only
Heroines and villains
The Earth Ones and the (Un)Heavenly Sent

CHOOSERS NOT LEADERS

All of the king's men but
None of the kingdom's voices

EXISTENCE

I thought about writing
A poem about feminism
Everything unapologetic
Everything strong women
Everything
WOMEN
WOMEN
WOMEN
Down to the tiny black dot

But then it dawned on me
That if there has to be
Another word for how historic
It is to be a woman living today
The question would not be
How far we've come or
How far we've yet to walk or
What laws want to know us or—

(You know the rest)

I thought to myself that maybe *woman* is also a verb

VALLEY WOMAN AND TRICKSTER SUN

Gold eggs led Her
To her grandmother's
One egg polite
One egg just right
But She got excited
She let that one tease her
She let that one run her away
So She walked all the way home with nothing
Not realizing until later it was just a trick of the Sun
Multiplying Himself in sets of four on the pavement

But little did Tricker Sun know She was The Light too
The next day on the way there She faced her palm to
the north
A burst of bright white light radiated from where She
stood and stretched all the way to the sky
And in the second's following She blinded his trickster
ass so good He turned from blue to white

That's why the Sun shines the color it is today

TRAGEDY

They buried
Spring in
A sarcophagus
At the base of
His ivory tower.

The flora
Line drawings:
Emerald.
The still face:
Blank, tan.

Stolen.

MOTHER UNIVERSE

Wildflowers
Rooted and died
Rooted and died again
Wherever she stepped;

The growth a
Quiet thundering
Of over two thousand
Suns destined to beige.

LIGHT IN THE DARK

I excel when I'm naturally me.
I don't need your #magic and I don't need your fancy
flora show.

But if you're still there when I'm down
And let me take in the grey for a little longer I'll know
you're a friend.

We were never meant to indefinitely shine through.
Don't you know stars get jealous of will-o'-the-wisps?

THE STARS START ON EARTH

Carefully I extend
My hand to touch
One of the five points of
This abandoned dream
Now caught in
Her bougainvillea bush.

I leave burned.

And we must call our own
Dreams down from the sky
We must hold our own net
And should we miss—we miss.
That's it.

AFTERTASTE

Diamonds are in everything
Even in waves
Even in moments
Even in tragedies

There's always a takeaway

MAD VALLEY YELLOW

The evening:
Tangerine like
April split open.

The valley:
Indented like
A false footprint.

TELEVISION

The hive cries
And the noise is divided
But the man is a quiet exterminator.

He's making honey from the passing hour.

WASHING AWAY

Falling into March's pool
Of strange chrysanthemums
I attempt to dive under the
White caps (white daisies)
But the wave closes its palm
And like an inescapable sheet
Collapsing softly...

                    softly...

                            softly...

March proves
It's serious about
Holding a mirror up to the clock
And succeeds in brushing my brown skin
With its pretty pinks and reds and oranges.

With the help of a blue glass sponge I wash the
minutes off.

STORY

I took the sun
And cracked it on
The kitchen counter.

Silky yellow-gold rivers
As thin as a strand of hair
Went everywhere and stained the floor.

I let the mess sit for over an hour.

A DISTANT LAND OF
NEVER-ENDING SIDEWAYS

The chaos was
Something of Monet.
The colors in that far section
Of the mountain range were
Exploding with different impressions
Of bronze and cerulean and vermillion.

And then there was the horizon.
Even without its sky sovereign the north
Had remained naked and low and pregnant with
The blues, in a suspicious way, as if it would crack in
two had either of us moved.

Spring grieved while autumn listened to our prayers.

EARTH LOVER

When
Earth
Was
Your
Emerald
Darling

SKY TAMERS

They made the sky wilt
Over itself like a petal in the rain—
Babied and unprepared for harsh weather
Yet so willing to be dressed head to toe in hibiscus.

But the text, they told us, was stolen many years ago.

THE NIGHTWALKER

So the sky cracked
(Or maybe it shattered
Everywhere and all at once)
And the pieces were picked up
Not by a poet but a nightwalker

MIRAGE

The plains spoke to us
In mirrored waves of lavender.
The flowers, open and full of the moon,
While the trees from trunk to leaf were
Aglow with the drunken language of the sun.

UNTIL

If this is the end
I won't have a clue
I don't keep track
Of goodbyes but
You can find me
Where the water
Waves back like clay
Remember my address
I live in the County of Blue

I want you to forget me but
I also hope you made your own with my colors
Just like I did yours

M . G . H U G H E S is a Black and Filipino poet and novelist based in San Diego, California. *I Only Have Marmalade* is her first book.

INSTAGRAM: @MGHUGHESAUTHOR
WEBSITE: MGHUGHESAUTHOR.COM

**MORE FROM
THOUGHT CATALOG BOOKS**

The Stength In Our Scars
—*Bianca Sparacino*

The Mountain Is You
—*Brianna Wiest*

Everything You'll Ever Need
(You Can Find Within Yourself)
—*Charlotte Freeman*

Your Heart Is The Sea
—*Nikita Gill*

**THOUGHT
CATALOG**
Books
THOUGHTCATALOG.COM
NEW YORK · LOS ANGELES